SUPER SAM

Written by Mary-Anne Creasy

Illustrated by Omar Aranda

Flying Start
to Literacy®

CONTENTS

CHAPTER 1:
A JOB FOR SAM

Sam was a superhero.

He had one super power – he could fly.

But Sam had a problem – he didn't have a job.

Superheroes had to have a job where they used their super powers. If they didn't, they would lose their super powers.

Sam had to find a job fast, so he flew off to look for one.

CHAPTER 2:
SAM TO THE RESCUE

Sam saw a house on fire.
There were flames and lots of smoke.

Firefighters were running into the house to save the people who were trapped.

"This looks like a job for Super Sam!"
said Sam. And he flew into the house.

There was so much smoke that he
couldn't see and he couldn't breathe.

A firefighter ran to Sam and carried him out of the house.

"What are you doing here, Sam?" said the firefighter.

"I wanted to rescue someone from the fire," said Sam.

"But you don't have a mask and an air tank," said the firefighter. "And you haven't been trained. You will have to find someone else to help."

So Sam flew off.

Sam was flying over the sea when he saw a rescue helicopter.

Suddenly, a rescue worker jumped out of the helicopter and swam to a man who was in the sea.

"This looks like a job for Super Sam!"
said Sam. And he flew into the sea.

But Sam couldn't swim.
"Help!" he called. "Help! Help!"

The rescue worker swam over to Sam
and pulled him up into the helicopter.

"Sam, what are you doing here?"
said the rescue worker.

"I wanted to help you," said Sam.

"But we had to help **you**, Sam," said the rescue worker. "Maybe you can find someone else to help."

So Sam flew off.

CHAPTER 3:
ONE MORE TRY

Sam was worried. He still didn't have a job.

As he flew over some mountains, he saw some rescue workers helping someone into a helicopter.

"Hey!" he shouted and waved. "I can help you!"

Sam landed on the snow. But the snow was soft. He went under the snow and he couldn't get out.

"Help!" he yelled.

A rescue worker quickly pulled
Sam out of the snow.

"What are you doing here, Sam?"
said the rescue worker.

"I wanted to help you," said Sam.
"I need a job or I will lose my
super power."

"Well, you can't work with us,"
said the rescue worker.
"We had to rescue **you**."

CHAPTER 4:
TIME TO GO HOME

Sam was ready to give up!

On the way home, he flew into a huge storm. Now he was wet! There was so much rain that the streets were flooded.

Suddenly, Sam saw a boy trapped in a
tree. The flood water was rising fast.
He flew over to the boy.

"I'm Super Sam and I can help you,"
said Sam. "Hold on!"

They flew over the town. The wind
was very strong and there was lots
and lots of rain.

Then, high up on a hill, Sam saw the rescue workers. Sam flew over to them.

"This is Super Sam," said the boy, "and he saved me."

"Sam, we need your help!" said the rescue workers. "The wind is strong and there is so much rain. Can you check that no one is trapped by the flood?"

"That sounds like a job for Super Sam!" said Sam. And off he flew.

All day, Sam rescued people who
were trapped by the flood.

Sam was a hero!

Now Sam has a job.

When there is a flood anywhere in the world, Super Sam is there to help!